CHIPPENHAM

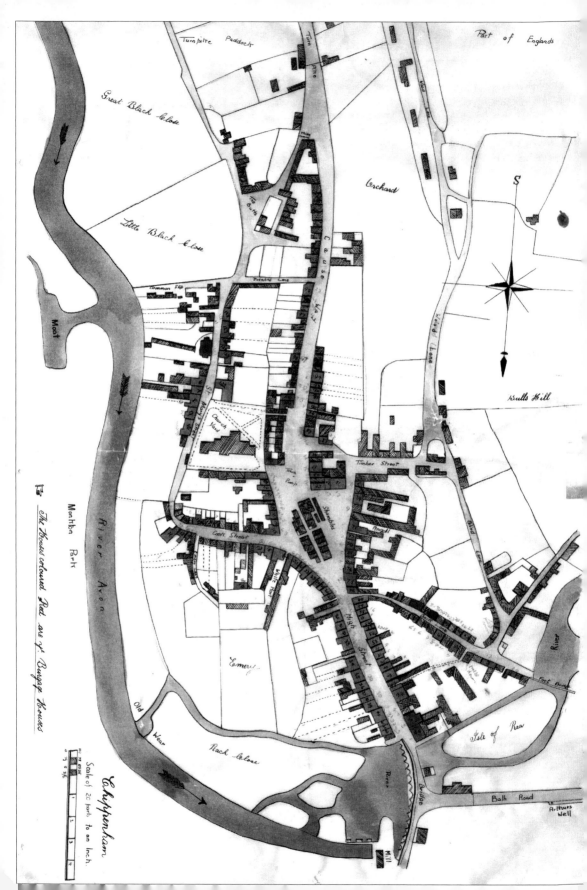

BRITAIN IN OLD PHOTOGRAPHS

CHIPPENHAM

MIKE STONE

Frontispiece: Map of Chippenham in 1800 showing the town centre.

Page three: Chippenham from the air in 1941.

View of Chippenham taken from the top of the Nestlé Milk Factory chimney in the 1920s.

First published in 2003 as part of the 'Images of England' series
This edition first published in 2009

Reprinted 2010, 2012

The History Press
The Mill, Brimscombe Port
Stroud, Gloucestershire, GL5 2QG
www.thehistorypress.co.uk

British Library Cataloguing in Publication Data.
A catalogue record for this book is available from the British Library.

ISBN 978 0 7524 5383 5

Typesetting and origination by The History Press
Printed in Great Britain by Marston Book Services Limited, Didcot

CONTENTS

ACKNOWLEDGEMENTS

The contents of this book could not have been compiled without the help of numerous people who have kindly loaned pictures and given historical details.

I would particularly like to thank David Affleck, Deirdre Clague, Elizabeth and Peter Hayes, Don Little, Philip Strand, Ivy Ward, Tony White, Annette Wilson and Doreen Wootton for photographs and historical and anecdotal details about the town of Chippenham. Further assistance was also given by Mike Brotherwood, Peggy Burgess, Beverley Hoff, Tam Pearce, Paul Salter and the staff of Chippenham Library.

A final thanks to my wife, Marilyn, for her able assistance in pulling the book together.

A Chippenham postman delivers to the town, c. 1890.

INTRODUCTION

The town of Chippenham is a prosperous and diverse growing community with new industries and an ever-increasing amount of new housing. The population has a strong community spirit, typified by regular events such as the Folk Festival, Millennium celebrations, Viking weekends, Eddie Cochrane weekend and a new arts festival.

The town and district councils, a thriving civic society and the efforts of many individuals have all combined to bring the heart back into the town. Important milestones have been the re-erection of the Butter Cross (1995), renovation of the Town Hall and Neeld Hall (1996), the new Chippenham Museum and Heritage Centre (2000), renovation of the Yelde Hall (2002) and many other projects. The town's heritage is being supported and appreciated along with a growing public demand for information about the town's historic past.

Only a handful of books and articles have been published on Chippenham's history and heritage in the nineteenth and twentieth centuries. Changing ideas and new facts help to flesh out the town's long history. In 1907 A.G. Bradley, in his book *Roundabout Wiltshire*, stated 'it is a place of ancient fame and a great deal might be said about it, if there were space in which to say it.' We still await a comprehensive history of Chippenham, although there is the excellent Butter Cross Bulletin, produced by the civic society, and shorter books continue to be published.

In 1957 the *Victoria County History for Wiltshire, Volume 1: Part 1* had no entries on the early history and archaeology of Chippenham. Between 1957 and 1975 many historic buildings, like the town mill and the town bridge, were swept away under modern re-developments. Planned excavations and chance finds have shown clearly that the core of the town on the spur of land, which is surrounded by the River Avon on three sides, had been attractive to prehistoric and Roman farmers. The town began to expand in the thirteenth century and continued to do so well into the fifteenth, occupying most of the spur of land within the horseshoe of the rivers with increased expansion along New Road over the bridge.

In 1928 Edward Hutton, in his book *Highways and Byways in Wiltshire*, stated that 'from the Conquest to the advent of the Great Western Railway, Chippenham, though on the Great Western Road, must be one of the sleepiest places in England'. Many authors concurred with this statement, few records survive to prove the contrary and there have been few large-scale excavations that might flesh out the town's later medieval history.

The wool industry grew in the sixteenth century, utilising the River Avon for power and the small islands along the river for drying the finished cloth on racks. In the seventeenth century the town suffered a recession in the wool industry along with the advent of outbreaks of plague and a drop in corn production. During the Civil War the cloth trade suffered due to the banning and disruption of the export of finished cloth to London. But in 1792 the town's burgesses cemented their fortunes in the wool industry by working with Sir Samuel Fludyer, who guaranteed their supplies of wool and a ready market for the finished cloth. The increased wealth of the burgesses was used to improve their town houses in the High Street, Market Place and St Mary's Street, using imported Bath stone and locally quarried stone, which resulted in Chippenham being called 'Little Bath'. In 1798 the town began a short flirtation with the Wiltshire and Berkshire canal and a branch was cut which terminated at the wharf, which is now the site of the bus station.

In 1841 the arrival of the Great Western Railway was said by many at the time to have 'awakened the town and its inhabitants'. This new transport system revitalised the cloth trade and in 1851 a first prize for cloth was awarded to the Chippenham weavers at the Great Exhibition in London.

The iron industry was also greatly influenced by the railway and extensive factories were constructed close to the railway line. In 1842 Roland Brotherhood set up his railway engineering works north of the station. In 1894 Evans O'Donnell took over part of his works and began to expand the factory, joining up with Saxby & Farmer in 1904. In 1920 they merged under the name of Westinghouse Brake & Saxby Signal Company Ltd, becoming Westinghouse Brake and Signal Company Ltd in 1935, the main employers in Chippenham for the twentieth century.

The celebrations in Chippenham for the Golden Jubilee of Queen Victoria in June 1887 involved most of the town's population, with a great ox roasting in the Market Place and the ringing of the church bells of St Andrew's, along with the issue of Jubilee medals from the mayor, Mr Edmund Awdry. In 1911 the Chippenham community celebrated the Coronation of King George V with a carnival, a huge bonfire and an illuminated procession through the main streets.

In 1914 the town council records describe the councillors trying to work out ways to ease the distress of the local people, whose men folk were fighting at the front in the First World War. The hardships of the war were observable to the town's population when wounded soldiers began to arrive at Neeld Hall, which was used as a hospital and treated about 1,800 wounded under the expert eye of the VAD nurses.

During the Second World War a platoon of local defence volunteers formed in Chippenham on 2 June 1940, who would later became the Home Guard. On the 20 April 1942 a bomb fell at the Folly in Bristol Road, probably dropped by a German plane on a night raid to Bath. On 8 May 1945 the Market Place and High Street were filled with the local community celebrating victory in Europe.

Chippenham's tradition of royal visits culminated in the visit of Her Majesty Queen Elizabeth II and Prince Philip on 7 December 2001, with the Duke visiting the new Museum & Heritage Centre and the Queen, after a short walk, visiting the Town Hall in the High Street.

Many members of Chippenham's community look back with fondness to the town before 1957, with the stone town bridge, the mill and a few medieval timber-framed buildings along with some imposing Georgian stone houses, all of which have sadly been demolished. What we have lost can still be enjoyed in the selection of pictures in this compilation. The town continues to grow with new industries, housing estates and roads. The population is now at the highest point in its entire history and further extensions are being planned to the town along with further redevelopment in the town centre. The town's heritage is secure and is increasingly appreciated with an ever-expanding archive, which is housed in the growing collections of the new Chippenham Museum & Heritage Centre.

ONE

HISTORY BEFORE
THE CAMERA

Early painting of the old Chippenham town bridge in 1792. The building with the weather vane was the old turnpike house, later known as Higgins' House, which was well known as one of the town's ironmonger shops. There was probably a timber bridge across the river from the ninth century, which may have been built of the stout oak that grew in the forests of Pewsham and Chippenham. The availability of local stone and the harsh winter floods probably prompted its re-construction in stone with piers and arches. The stone bridge was regularly strengthened, repaired and widened to accommodate the increased traffic. By 1800 coaches were passing freely over the bridge. The gates to the left of the bridge led down to the island of Rea, where the town's hunting dogs were kept in kennels. The bridge was eventually demolished and replaced by a new bridge, which was officially opened on 2 May 1966.

Watercolour painting dated about 1880 showing the original position of the Butter Cross, with the butcher's shambles to the right. On the left of the picture the Three Cups Inn is shown, which changed its name to the Talbot. In 1889 the Butter Cross was taken down and re-erected in the grounds of the manor, Castle Combe. The Butter Cross has now been brought back to Chippenham and was erected in the centre of the market place in 1995.

15 GUINEAS
REWARD.

WHEREAS on the Night of Friday or Saturday last,

A FAT WETHER
SHEEP,

the property of Mr. **THOMAS RUMMING**, of Showell
Farm, in the Parish of Lacock, was feloniously

KILLED AND CARRIED AWAY.

This is to give Notice,

that any person or persons who will give such Information as may lead to the Conviction of the Offender or
Offenders shall receive the Sum of **TEN GUINEAS**
from the said THOMAS RUMMING, and the further Sum of
FIVE GUINEAS from the Lacock Prosecution Society,
by applying to Mr. **W. AWDRY**, Solicitor, Chippenham.

Chippenham, Feb. 3rd, 1834.

ALEXANDER, PRINTER AND BOOKBINDER, CHIPPENHAM.

A poster dated 1834, detailing the killing of a 'fat wether sheep'. Numerous records survive offering rewards along with fines for felons, who were rustling and killing animals that were intended for the important markets in Chippenham. Ownership of the market rights was of considerable value to the lord of the manors, who also had control of the space in front of all the premises in the market place. In 1765 all farmers in Chippenham were ordered to bring their corn, butter, cheese, turkeys, geese, chickens, pigeons, conies, eggs and all other dead victuals to sell in the public market, and by 1792 there was a considerable amount of corn being sold in the market in Saturdays. With the opening of the new Town Hall by Joseph Neeld the corn was sold in the Exchange at the rear. There are three interesting paintings of the market in process by Louise Rayner, who exhibited at the Royal Academy in 1865. They show a packed market day with stalls loaded with produce and buskers entertaining the crowds.

A print published by Mr Noyes in 1863, showing the centre of Chippenham from the sides of the new railway embankment. The roofed railway station can be seen on the far left leading out onto Station Hill, which had yet to be developed. The first building to be erected was the Baptist

chapel, which stood for a few years on its own until further buildings were erected on Station Hill. Running behind Station Hill can be seen the buildings of St Mary's Place. The spire of St Andrew's church is clearly visible, with the High Street leading down towards the bridge.

A print by Mr Noyes from around the 1860s, showing the centre of Chippenham across the river, with the town surrounded by open countryside. Views of Chippenham from the countryside were a popular choice for local artists, particularly J.H. Joliffe, who painted over fifty views from 1868.

Pencil drawing of the north end of the Market Place, c. 1850. The pens for the animals can be seen on the left with a man carrying buckets towards the town well, which is just off picture. The buildings on the right were used as a series of public houses from the eighteenth century until the nineteenth century.

TWO

AT THE MARKET

Market day at the top end of the market, with the sale in progress of cattle in 1904. In 1907 the Board of Agriculture prohibited on-street cattle markets. The market relocated to the rear of the Neeld Hall in 1910 and then to a new purpose-built cattle market near the railway station in 1954.

Market day outside the Bear Hotel where the sale of horses is taking place, in the 1890s.

Market day in about 1870, where cows are being driven in front of the old Yelde Hall, which was then the fire station run by Captain David Baigent.

The Market Place in 1875 with the town fountain and pump, which sits above the town well. Hauliers are sat on their wagons awaiting their loads, which will be carried off at the end of market day.

The Market Place on a non-market day. On the left is the Duke of Cumberland, which prior to 1750 was known as The Trooper. Next is the spirit vaults and on the end is the Kings Head Inn, with St Andrew's church hidden behind Smalcomb's, furniture removers. The added eighteenth-century front façade of Smalcomb's hides the Tudor box-frame building. In 1613 this building was occupied by the Lyon Inn. An interesting story is often related that in early 1666 John Woodman is supposed to have plotted with others to start what became the Great Fire of London.

The top end of the Market Place in about 1915 with Ball's hairdressing salon, which occupies the ground floor of a Tudor timber building. The English Colonial Meat Company was built into the façade of a late Georgian town house, which is now occupied by a fish and chip shop. Penny & Son, the fish and chip café, is one of the ever-growing numbers of fast-food takeaways. The corner shop of John Coles was a chemist and wine and spirit merchant and was opened in the 1870s. He produced his own patent medicines and recommended many invalid wines such as Spanish port, Quinnie wine and Coca wine to improve his customers health. In 1891, 1896 and 1915 John Coles was elected Mayor of Chippenham. He died in the following year and left a legacy to the borough council, to be used for educational and recreational purposes. The borough council invested the legacy and, along with loans, purchased and developed fifteen acres of parkland, which was opened to the public on 23 May 1923.

The Butter Cross in around 1890, showing its plain Doric columns and the stone-tiled roof, which is in a poor state of repair. The buildings behind backed onto the Yelde Hall in the 1780s. Running along in front of the Butter Cross, and up to the corner where the old Waverley Café stood, was a roofed building with no sides which contained a long bench on which all the slaughtered cattle, pigs and sheep were cut up for all the nearby butcher's shops in the market.

The position of the Butter Cross can be clearly seen in this rare view taken in around 1899. The Butter Cross is hemmed in by the Victorian buildings which replaced late Tudor stone and timber buildings, which were associated with the butchery trade in the centre of the market place.

The shop front of the Wiltshire Bacon Company in around 1980, showing the famous joints of bacon hanging in the window.

A public auction in the 1920s outside the Kings Head Inn.

THREE

HIGH STREET, BRIDGE AND THE FLOODS

View down the High Street in 1920, with the impressive burgage houses and banks on the right.

Early view of the High Street in about 1860. The shop front of Houlston's Library can be seen on the left and then the premises of John Gantlett, a watchmaker. He was born in Calne in 1843, the son of Quintillian and Elizabeth. In the 1891 census he was also described as being a gold jeweller. The Gantlett family also made clocks and watches in Great Sherston and Church Street, Calne.

View of the front of Blackfords Ironmongers, which is in the process of being demolished in 1908. The building had been restored in 1761 and was probably built in the Tudor period.

View looking down the High Street towards the bridge in about 1890. The façade of the Town Hall can be seen with its flagpole above. The two imposing Bath stone buildings with their plain Georgian façades were built as town houses by the burgesses using profits from the weaving trade. Like many other town houses in the High Street they gradually were turned into shops and businesses from about 1850. The site of the town hall building by Joseph Neeld in 1834 occupies an area of land which from 1785 was occupied by the Antelope Inn. Records from 1666 also indicate the existence of the Canon Inn.

View down the High Street in 1890 showing the wide range of shops and businesses. Behind the posed children is one of the many milk carts, which delivered milk to the town tradesmen.

View up the High Street in the early 1900s. The postman on the right stands near the front of the Co-operative Society, which was active from 1907 and ceased trading in Chippenham in the 1990s. On the right of the High Street the imposing façade of the Town Hall can be seen. The classical arch with the Borough coat of arms, carved in stone above, leads into the markets, which were erected by Joseph Neeld in the middle of the nineteenth century. Produce sold consisted mainly of cheese and corn. In 1872 cheese sales reached 1,856 tons, but by 1884 it had dropped to 984 tons. The arch has been recently cleaned and now leads into the new shopping precinct.

Opposite above: East side of the High Street in the 1920s. The two stone buildings on the right-hand side of the picture have been demolished and now form the entrance to Emery Gate shopping centre.

Opposite below: Picture taken in the 1920s of the imposing Palladian revival house of Mr G.A. White. The building may have been designed by John Wood, the Elder, of Bath in the eighteenth century. The building was originally erected at Bowdon Hill in about 1744 and later rebuilt at 24 High Street, Chippenham. The building was again demolished in 1932 and was skilfully taken down and re-erected at 1 Sion Hill, Bath, which is now part of Kingswood school. It has been described as a 'poem in masonry' and this house, along with the other Bath stone buildings, was the reason why Chippenham was called 'Little Bath' in the eighteenth century.

Two Tudor period timber-framed buildings in the late 1940s, which have since been demolished. The fishmongers and poulterers was run by Mr Holland in 1891 until 1901 when it was taken over by Mr Hiscock and Joseph Buckle, who ran a very successful business, described by one of their admirers as 'Chippenham's own little Harrods'. Joe Buckle was involved in many aspects of sport in the town and was also captain of the Chippenham town fire brigade. He also began to amass a large collection of insurance fire badges, which he displayed towards the rear of his shop front. He was always pleased to show them off to anyone, but perhaps his most famous visitor was Queen Mary in 1943, who upon arrival at the front of his shop was duly given a guided tour by Joe Buckle.

View of the end of River Street with the back bridge over the River Avon in about 1903. In the early 1970s the whole of River Street and its buildings was swept away for the development of Sainsbury's supermarket and other retail outlets. These too have now been demolished and replaced with the precinct shopping centre.

Above: View up the High Street in about 1906 before the erection of the Co-op on the left-hand side of the picture. The low-roofed building behind the end of the bridge balustrade was occupied by Thomas Trotman as a studio photographer.

Right: River Street in around 1908 showing the Lamb Inn and next to it the shotgun factory of Mr Warrilow, who set up his factory here in the 1880s in the old Spiers silk building. He produced universal double-breach loader shotguns, which he patented and won a silver medal for. He also made the universal hammerless gun, the Acme sportsman's gun and a wide selection of shotgun cartridges. Most of his shotguns were sold to the gentry around Chippenham. Mr Warrilow also kept up with the fashion by setting up his own shooting school at Westmead and held shooting demonstrations at the great estates nearby.

View of the stone bridge, which crosses the River Avon, in the late 1950s before it was demolished and replaced by the new town bridge in 1966.

View of the disastrous floods of 1893.

Wagons and people standing above the top of the flood in 1903.

View across the meadows to the rear of Waterford Mill on the third day of the flood, 17 June 1903.

View from the High Street near the Town Hall in January 1926.

People being ferried across the floods in 1926 for a small charge, here passing by the front of the Co-op.

View of the floods on 2 May 1932, from the top of 27 High Street.

The old town bridge, the view here displaying some of its twenty-two stone arches. In 1613 William Bollyn was paid £3 16s for nineteen loads of hewed stone to make arches, as part of the bridge had fallen down. In 1615 the bridge actually collapsed, and it was then not until 1641 that repairs were fairly advanced to bring the bridge back to public use. In 1684 the 'Great Frost' caused a build up of ice on the upside of the arches, and teams of men were employed to break it and push it through. Then in 1796 the bridge was finally widened along its whole length, making it a suitable pathway for the ever-increasing traffic, after a meeting in the Yelde Hall resolved to spend a large amount of money on the project.

FOUR

CIVIC PRIDE

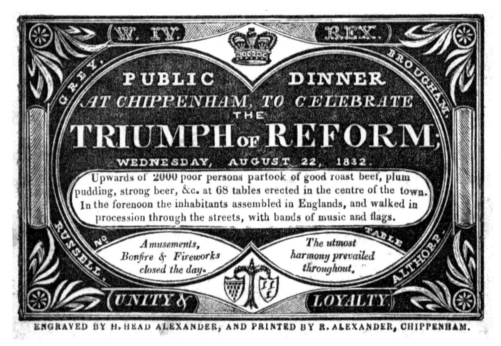

Commemorative card to record the important public dinner on Wednesday 22 August 1832, with the 2,000 persons who partook of a good roast dinner after the government's triumph of the Great Reform Act.

The old Town Hall in the 1890s when it was used as the headquarters of the Volunteer Rifle Corps until 1911. Above the door is the coat of arms of the town, which commemorates the building's use as the Town Hall and market building from the fifteenth century up until 1841.

View of the interior of the upper floor council chamber in Yelde Hall, where the bailiffs and burgesses held council.

JAMES THOMSON, ARCH.T   DEL. ET LITH.

THE·NEW·HALL·AND·MARKET·PLACE.
ERECTED·AT·CHIPPENHAM· WILTS· AD 1833.
JOSEPH NEELD ESQ.RE M.P.

Joseph Neeld, who was MP for Chippenham, paid for the erection of the new Town Hall in 1833, where the mayor and councillors met to run the town. The area under the arches was used for storage and for retail sales.

An imposing picture of Chas B. Pollard, who was mace-bearer to the mayor and councillors in 1897. The mace was presented by Joseph Neeld in 1844.

Signed polling card for Captain Cazalet, who was elected Conservative MP for Chippenham, 14 November 1935. On the 4 July 1943 he was killed in a flying accident at Gibralter, along with General Sikorski, in mysterious circumstances.

POLLING DAY

THURSDAY, Nov. 14th, 1935.

YOUR VOTE FOR

PROGRESS and PROSPERITY

is asked for Captain

CAZALET

The National Conservative Candidate.

Our Country's position is still too serious for party strife.

Things have improved vastly in the last four years—let this continue.

A return to Socialist Government means financial chaos.

There cann.; be a Liberal Government therefore—

VOTE NATIONAL.

Above: View looking up the High Street showing the arrival of Mr Neeld in 1850, to commemorate the enlargement of the Town Hall and the cheese market behind.

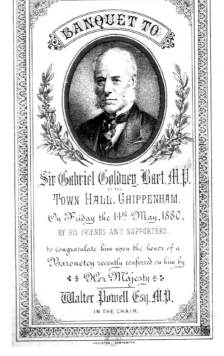

BANQUET TO

Sir Gabriel Goldney, Bart. M.P.
AT THE
TOWN HALL, CHIPPENHAM,
On Friday the 14th May, 1880,
BY HIS FRIENDS AND SUPPORTERS.

to congratulate him upon the honor of a
Baronetcy recently conferred on him by
★ Her Majesty ★

Walter Powell Esq. M.P.
IN THE CHAIR.

Souvenir to commemorate the conferred baronetcy on Sir Gabriel Goldney, MP for Chippenham, on 14 May 1880.

CHIPPENHAM
WATER
Supply Company Limited.

Having been requested to convene a Public Meeting of the Inhabitants of Chippenham and its immediate Neighbourhood, for the purpose of establishing a Company for the supply of pure and wholesome Water for domestic and general purposes, flushing Sewers, and for immediate use in case of Fire:

I hereby give Notice, that a

PUBLIC MEETING

will be holden at the TOWN HALL, Chippenham, on FRIDAY next, the 27th instant, at Seven o'clock in the Evening, and it is hoped the Meeting will be well attended.

Thos. Abdy Fellowes,
MAYOR.

SEPTEMBER 23rd, 1867.

Poster dated 23 September 1867, calling for a public meeting in order to improve the town's water and sewage systems.

FIVE

CHURCH
AND CHAPEL

St Andrew's church in the 1880s with the fine iron railings
surrounding the church, which were removed during the
Second World War for recycling.

Interior of St Andrew's church in 1875, showing the fine Norman arch, which was relocated in the 1878 restoration and rebuilding programme.

View of St Andrew's church in 1875 showing the beginning of the demolition of the east end prior to rebuilding. The church was built on an outcrop of rock and stands high above St Mary's Street with its view down to the River Avon. The line of the wall at the rear of the church is thought by many to be the line of the defences erected in the ninth century by the Saxons and the Danes.

St Andrew's church bells, removed for re-hanging in 1950. Left to right: H. Marsh; C. Bridgman; T. Davison; W. Thorold (foreman bell-hanger); H. Heath; S. Wiltshire (tower captain & ringing master); B. Hulbert (verger).

View across the river in the 1900s showing the east end of St Andrew's church and the Church school.

Opposite: St Paul's church, Chippenham, in the 1890s. It was designed by the famous national architect Sir George Gilbert Scott (who also designed eleven other buildings in Wiltshire). The building was started in 1853 and was built by Daniel Jones, a builder from Bradford-on-Avon. The church was finished in 1861 and was consecrated in 1855. In 1911 the architect Sir Harold Brakespear built the stone reredos and H. Gaye built the choir vestry, along with the organ chamber extension. In 1915 the church called in Hadden & Co., heating engineers of Trowbridge, to install a heating apparatus into the large draughty church. In 1955 Oswald Brakespear, who was in architectural practice in Corsham and the son of Sir Harold Brakespear, built the church baptistry and H.R. Hunt, a carpenter, installed the choir stalls.

Church of St Nicholas, Hardenhuish, which was erected in 1779 by Joseph Colborne. The church was designed by John Wood, the famous Bath classical architect, whose best-known work is the Royal Crescent.

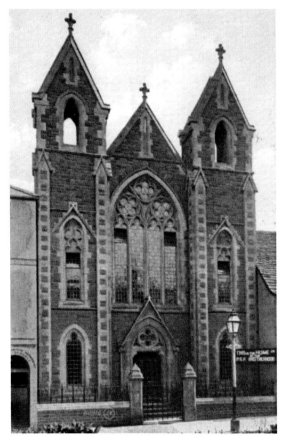

Left: Primitive Methodist church in the Causeway, Chippenham, founded in 1853. The church survives and is now used as a music and singing centre.

Below: The new Wesleyan church on the slopes of Monkton Hill was erected on the site of the Black Horse Inn, which was first recorded in documents in 1784. Nearby was a small pottery workshop producing earthenware pots for sale in the town. The land was bought in 1900 and was cleared and excavated between 1902 and 1903 by the men of the church. The building was opened in 1909 and was intended to mark the centenary of Methodism in Chippenham.

SIX

TRADE AND INDUSTRY

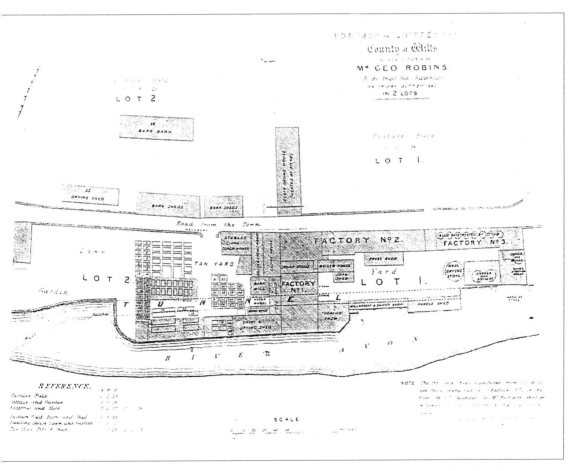

Sale plan of the Waterford Cloth Mill and Chippenham Tannery, which was up for sale in lots at the Angel Hotel on Friday 21 October 1842.

View along the central courtyard of Waterford Cloth Mill in the 1850s, with the tidy piles of equipment during a refurbishment.

The workforce of the Waterford Cloth Mill in around 1910. The factory is mentioned in the town rates in 1811 and was owned by George Austin & Co. By 1814 the factory was owned by Thomas Bailey, who also owned the tannery adjoining it. In 1815 Bailey sold the factory with its water wheel, steam engine, mill tackle, counting house, dye house and drying stove to John Saunders, Thomas Saunders and Charles Salter Taylor, for £460. The principle building, seen behind the workforce, was of five storeys, fifty feet by thirty-six feet with a powerful water wheel, driven by two Boulton and Watt engines. These drove on the ground floor ten pairs of fulling stocks, five broad and two narrow gigs, six indigo pots, six scribbling and four carding engines, and eighteen shearing frames. The factory at its height of production was capable of producing twenty-five pieces or fifty ends of broadcloth a week.

A new Lancashire boiler towed by a traction engine en route, probably, to the Waterford Cloth Mill in the 1890s.

The workforce standing in front of the tan pits holding their tools of trade at the rear of Chippenham Tannery, which opened in 1861 and was owned by Messrs J. and T.A. Smith. The tannery closed in 1928 and the buildings were used by Flowers, the scrap merchants. Adjoining this tannery was a further tannery, which was owned by Thomas Bailey and in use by 1814. All that survives of the tannery buildings today is the brick chimney next to the oak bark store and the rows of tanning pits dug into the ground.

Early photograph in the 1870s of the Bridge Cloth Factory, which started business in 1796, when Henry Burnet sold a leasehold house near the bridge to Thomas Goldney. In the rate books of 1811 the factory is described as having a dye house and shear shops. The Goldney family were prominent clothiers in the town from the sixteenth century right up to the nineteenth century. In 1818 the factory became the property of Anthony Guy, who was a lawyer and banker, but he was declared bankrupt in 1830. It was then sold to Joseph Spears with a twenty-one year lease and used for a short while as a silk factory. In 1873 the factory was taken over by the National Anglo-Swiss Milk Company.

View across the River Avon of the converted Bridge Cloth Factory into the National Anglo-Swiss Milk Company in the 1880s. The condensed milk factory is probably the oldest condensery in England and was the first factory to have installed a modern stainless steel plant and machinery in 1935. The factory was the largest employer in the town and in 1905 a merger took place between the Anglo-Swiss and the Henri Nestlé company to become the Nestlé and Anglo-Swiss Condensed Milk Factory. The Swiss chalet-style building, known as Bank House, was built originally as the milk company's offices; when it is compared to architects' drawings it appears never to have been fully completed. In the 1880s the Chippenham factory was beginning to suffer from competition from the Wilts United Dairies in Melksham, which was to become the giant Unigate Company. In 1897 the Anglo-Swiss opened a further factory at Staverton near Trowbridge, which is still in existence.

The daily arrival of milk entering Nestlé Milk Factory in the 1890s. Records of work at the factory survive and describe it as being extremely hard. Work commenced sharply at 6 a.m. and finished at 7 p.m. In 1873 the ten-hour working day earned four shillings a week. Workers were summoned by a single bell housed on the roof of the factory in a small turret, which still survives. The well-known milk products from the factory were labelled 'Milk Maid sweetened condensed milk'. In the Second World War Red Cross parcels were packed at the Chippenham factory and despatched as far afield as Australia. The condensery finally closed in 1962 when production was transferred to a new Nestlé factory in Cumberland.

Damaged view looking along the front of the Nestlé Milk Factory with a bank house on the left.

Picture of the grand opening of the cheese market on 12 September 1850, with numerous wagons being loaded with Wiltshire cheese for distribution to its customers.

Interior view of the cheese and corn exchange market in 1896 with the council officials and cheese dealers and members of the public standing. The cheese market survives and and is now used as a function suite by Chippenham Town Council.

Interior of premises used by the Royal Wilts Bacon Company Limited for the temporary storage of ninety-six packing cases of Wiltshire cheese, which will be shipped to the Coronation Durbar of King George V in Delhi, India, in 1911.

The front of the town mill in 1905, which was run by the Collen brothers. The earliest known record of mills in Chippenham is the Doomsday Survey of 1086, where twelve mills are recorded with a value of £6. From 1671 the mill belonged to the Baynton's of Spye Park and then from 1800 to Mr Edridge of Monkton, who in turn sold it in 1810. In 1816 a fire destroyed the mill. It was rebuilt after 1817 and was run by a sixteen-feet wide breast shot waterwheel, which provided power for turning nine pairs of mill stones. In 1957 the mill was demolished and the site has been redeveloped for retail shops. A good deal of the demolished building materials from the mill were recycled. There is also a record from Mr Walker that two pairs of French burr stones for grinding were sold on to a firm in Southern Rhodesia and were used to grind groundnuts!

Humphries & Sons,

Contractors for all Classes of Rolling Stock for Agricultural and Trade Purposes.

Trade advert for Humphries & Sons, the largest wagon works in Chippenham, which began in the mid-Victorian period and successfully traded until 1946, when William Humphries joined business with Hector Simons and they formed an engineering company, which lasted until 1999, when it went into voluntary liquidation.

Trade picture of one of the many types of carrying wagon that Humphries built in the wagon works in the Causeway, Chippenham.

F. A. MACKNESS,

COACH MAKER,
and all Motor Coach Works.

MOTOR CANOPIES, WIND SCREENS, Etc.

PAINTING and TRIMMING EXECUTED AT SHORTEST NOTICE.

We also make a Speciality of a most Comfortable Governess Car with improved Driving Seat and all with Rubber Tyres.

Trade advert for F.A. Mackness, coach-maker, who had his premises behind the White Hart Inn, which is now the Iceland food store.

Workers at Humphries wagon works in the Causeway with their tools of trade and the workshop dog, in around the 1880s.

Flat wagon made by Chequers at their factory behind Tugela Road, c. 1900.

Portrait of William Goold Slade, the son of Richard Slade, who founded Slade's Brewery with its brewing premises in Union Road.

AND DIRECTORY ADVERTISER.

ESTABLISHED OVER HALF A CENTURY.

SLADE & SONS,

BREWERS.

HIGH-CLASS PALE ALES

Special Invalid Stout.

Price List on Application.

PURE ÆRATED WATERS

IN CORKED AND PATENT BOTTLES.

SPECIALITY:

DRY GINGER ALE,

PROMPT ATTENTION Given to all Orders by Post.

ADDRESS:

Brewery, Chippenham.

Trade advertisement for Slade's Brewery in Union Road, dated 1913.

Interior of the brewery in Union Road in the early 1920s. In about 1898 Llewellins and James of Bristol installed new brewery fittings along with white glazed bricks in the cooling rooms.

Delivery of the barrels of beer from the brewery houses of Union Road to the tied houses in Chippenham, which were the following: the Five Alls in the Causeway; New Road Inn; Royal Oak in London Road; Railway Inn in Union Road; the Pack Horse in London Road and the Woolpack in River Street.

Above: Brewers at the rear of Slade's Brewery, Union Road with the delivery drays behind, *c.* 1910.

Front cover of the closing down sale of Slade's Brewery on 21 July 1926.

The canal wharf in around 1870, with the barge *Helen* and John Trow at the tiller. Standing at the rear is Mr W.H. Brinkworth, who owned most of the trade contracts on the spur of the Wiltshire and Berkshire canal. In the *Town Council Records*, dated 8 February 1794, a plan was presented to the bailiff and burgesses for bringing a canal into Chippenham. The purpose of the canal was to bring coal from Somerset and return with agricultural products. The canal cut was dug in 1798 and in 1799 the town bailiff received £259 9s 8d from the canal company agent to cover the cost of two and a half acres of land. The arrival of the railways in 1841 began the loss of trade and money for the shareholders. In 1917 Chippenham Town Council gave permission for the canal from the tunnel to the wharf to be filled in.

CHIPPENHAM WHARF WEIGHING ENGINE,
ALSO DEPOT AT GREAT WESTERN RAILWAY STATION.

Mr. *E. Slade*   *Nov* 30   1875

Bought of W. H. BRINKWORTH,

COAL & SLATE MERCHANT, &c.

BRICK, TILE, AND PIPE MANUFACTURER, POTTER, &c.

Trader in Stourbridge, Staffordshire, & Bridgewater Goods for Building purposes.   The Trade supplied.

S. SPINKS, PRINTER, CHIPPENHAM.

	T.	C.	Qr.		£	s.	d.
To *1000 × 2in pot pipes*							
Gross							
Tare							
Net				at			

Witness, *W. H. B*

A receipt for clay pipes from Brinkworth's to Mr E. Slade, dated 30 November 1875.

Hathaways'
END OVER END CHURNS
FITTED WITH NEW
Instantaneous Cantilever Cover Fasteners

Power without effort. No wearing parts to replace.

Each Fastener fitted with automatic lubricator.

Churns in present use can be fitted with these

fasteners. Eccentric Action. New Safety Cover Rest.

Hygienic Air Valve.   Improved Eyelet.

Best and Cheapest on the Market.

Hathaways'
CELEBRATED " SHAKESPEARIAN "

End ——
Over End
——Churns

Fitted with Cover Fasteners, Tinned Steel Clips and Screws.
SIZES and PRICES.

SIZE OF CHURN.		Holds when full imp gals	Maximum Butter Produced.	PRICE
No.				£ s. d.
1A	Household Churn (on low stand for table)	3	5 lbs.	4 0 0
1	(on anti-friction rollers and high stand)	5	7 lbs.	5 1 6
2	"	8	12 lbs.	6 3 6
3	"	12	18 lbs.	6 17 0
4	"	16	25 lbs.	7 15 0
5	"	25	39 lbs.	9 5 0
6	"	32	50 lbs.	10 5 0
7	"	44	66 lbs.	11 17 3
8	"	52	78 lbs.	12 15 3
9	"	70	105 lbs.	14 16 0
10	"	77	114 lbs.	15 12 3
11	"	100	150 lbs.	18 6 0

All sizes fitted with Eccentric Action and Gun Metal Ring in end.

Sale catalogue of the celebrated Hathaway's household barrel churns, end-over churns and butter workers that were made in the factory on the corner of Foundry Lane and Old Road for 1934. The factory was established in 1869 and won many medals for products that were of a very high standard. The family firm manufactured many thousands of butter churns both for the market in this country and for the wider market of the British Empire. Nicholas Hathaway was also a trained and skilled motor engineer importing French cars, which he then customised and sold on. The machinery he used for customising and repairing cars was used in the First World War for manufacturing munitions. By 1934 the bulk manufacturing of butter caused a severe drop in the sales of butter churns.

Hathaways'
CELEBRATED " SHAKESPEARIAN "
End Over End
HOUSEHOLD CHURN

This Handy little Churn is fitted with Eccentric Action and specially adapted for making small quantities from ¼ to 5 lbs. and will produce butter much superior to that made in any Box Churn, and is also a far better investment, lasting a life-time if properly looked after. The Churn and Stand takes up very little space, and when not in use can be placed under the table.

Front cover of the sale catalogue of the contents of Hathaway's Factory, which was sold by auction on the 12 November 1937.

Below and opposite: Three panels from the advertising poster for the Simplex patent carpet sweeper that was produced in Hathaway's Factory in 1934 in order to keep the business going.

HATHAWAY'S NEW SIMPLEX
(PATENT)
KING, QUEEN AND EMPEROR
CARPET SWEEPERS

ARE THE MOST EFFICIENT SWEEPING MACHINES NOW MANUFACTURED, AND INCORPORATE MANY OUTSTANDING IMPROVEMENTS, AS SET OUT BELOW.

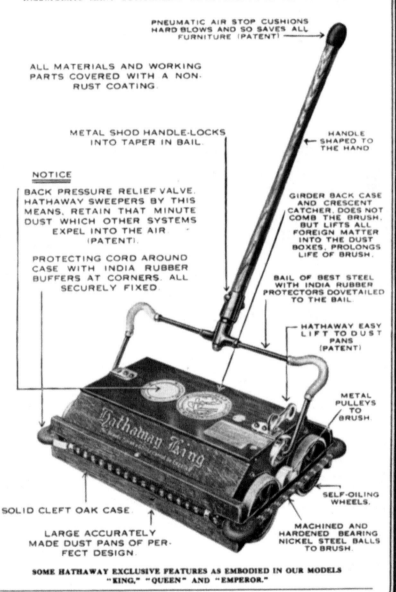

PNEUMATIC AIR STOP CUSHIONS HARD BLOWS AND SO SAVES ALL FURNITURE (PATENT)

ALL MATERIALS AND WORKING PARTS COVERED WITH A NON-RUST COATING.

HANDLE SHAPED TO THE HAND

METAL SHOD HANDLE-LOCKS INTO TAPER IN BAIL.

NOTICE

BACK PRESSURE RELIEF VALVE. HATHAWAY SWEEPERS BY THIS MEANS, RETAIN THAT MINUTE DUST WHICH OTHER SYSTEMS EXPEL INTO THE AIR. (PATENT).

PROTECTING CORD AROUND CASE WITH INDIA RUBBER BUFFERS AT CORNERS. ALL SECURELY FIXED.

GIRDER BACK CASE AND CRESCENT CATCHER. DOES NOT COMB THE BRUSH, BUT LIFTS ALL FOREIGN MATTER INTO THE DUST BOXES, PROLONGS LIFE OF BRUSH.

BAIL OF BEST STEEL WITH INDIA RUBBER PROTECTORS DOVETAILED TO THE BAIL.

HATHAWAY EASY LIFT TO DUST PANS (PATENT)

METAL PULLEYS TO BRUSH.

SELF-OILING WHEELS.

SOLID CLEFT OAK CASE.

LARGE ACCURATELY MADE DUST PANS OF PERFECT DESIGN.

MACHINED AND HARDENED BEARING NICKEL STEEL BALLS TO BRUSH.

SOME HATHAWAY EXCLUSIVE FEATURES AS EMBODIED IN OUR MODELS "KING," "QUEEN" AND "EMPEROR."

"THEY KEEP THE HOME YOUNG"

Letterhead of Samuel Spink, printer, who set up his printing works in the Causeway, with a shop in the Market Place in 1858.

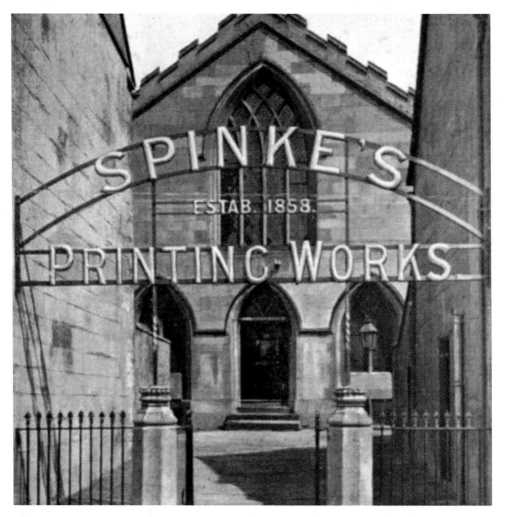

The imposing entrance to the new printing works set up in the Causeway chapel in 1909.

The interior of the composing room in the old chapel, 1909.

The machine room in the basement of the old chapel, 1909.

Above: The retail shop of Spink's printing works in the Market Place, 1909.

SMALL'S Stationery Stores and Newsagency, Market Place, CHIPPENHAM.

Picture Post-cards in great variety. New Local Views are constantly being added to our stock.
Grafton China bearing Chippenham Borough Arms, a variety of designs, from **6d.** each.
We also sell Cigarettes and Packet Tobaccos.
The favour of your kind patronage is respectfully solicited.

Trade advert for Small's, the stationery stores in the Market Place, Chippenham, c. 1890, from the *Chippenham Borough Guide* published by Mr Houlston.

Letterhead of the Wiltshire Bacon Company Limited, which set up business in the old Brotherhood's foundry in Foundry Road in the late nineteenth century and was one of the largest curing factories with a capacity of over 150 pigs per week.

Interior of the old Brotherhood's foundry building showing the cured bacon.

F.W. Teagle, *Chippenham.*
BUTCHER,
National Telephone No. 7X.
Families waited on daily for orders.
BEST QUALITY IS TRUE ECONOMY.

Trade advert for Mr Teagle, butcher, *c.* 1890, displaying his meat in his shop at 49 New Road.

For Antique and Modern Furniture go to
F. G. BEAVEN, 30, Market Place, Chippenham. The Stock comprises Dining and Drawing Room Suites, Wardrobes, Overmantels, Tables Couches, Chairs, Clocks, Timepieces, Glass, China, Fenders and Irons, Bedsteads and Bedding, Prints, Engravings, Oil Paintings, etc., etc.
Furniture Removed and Warehoused.

Trade advert for Beavan & Son, who sold antique and modern furniture, *c.* 1890.

Trade advert for Edgar Neale, chemist at 10 High Street, who set up business in 1879. Neale made and sold many medicines, along with the fashionable mineral waters and a wide variety of invalid jellies, of which turtle was very popular. Along with many other chemists he also began to be involved with the popular hobby of photography, supplying plates, films and cameras and also a dark room for use by amateurs.

Trade advert for Arthur Spencer, who ran a music warehouse at 13 Market Place, from 1883 to 1950. In the early 1900s the shop specialised in musical instruments and the latest phonographs and gramophones. By about 1930 he was also selling the latest radiograms and wireless sets.

Trade advert for Frank Belcher, family drapers and outfitters in the Market Place, in around 1890.

Opposite below: The shop front of A.R. Hinder, who sold cycles and motorcycles in the shop built into the front of Orwell House next to the railway viaduct, in 1922.

Trade advert for Hetherington & Son at 8 High Street, who specialised in clothes for ladies and gentlemen's leisure activities, from the 1870s until the1950s. Ralph Hetherington and his son John were tailors to the local gentry and made and supplied most of the livery for the footmen, coachmen and grooms for the Spicers of Spye Park, the Lansdownes of Bowood and the Clutterbucks of Hardenhuish. They also made hunting outfits for the Duke of Beaufort and the Avonvale Hunts. Graham Hetherington owned a livery stable at the rear of 8 High Street, supplying horses to the Wilts Yeomanry. During the First World War he brought mules and horses to Europe from South America and for these services he was awarded the MBE.

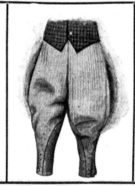

HETHERINGTON & SON,
Ladies' and Gent.'s Tailors.

Cycling and Walking Costumes, Liveries.

Hunting, Sporting, Clerical, and Motor Suits

. . Breeches a Speciality. . .

8, High Street, Chippenham.

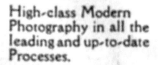

Above: Trade advert for Porter's the artist photographers, at 11 Lands End, *c.* 1890.

Trade advert for James Witts, upholsterer and furniture repair shop in the Market Place, in around 1890.

Ironmongers shop of W. Gardner, at 6 High Street in 1890. Many of the hand tools are displayed outside the shop, on the pavement and leaning against the Town Hall next door.

ROBT. AFFLECK,

Manufacturing, Furnishing, General Ironmonger and Sports Agent.

Brazier, tin and iron plate worker, bell-hanger, gas fitter and whitesmith. Stoves, Grates and Kitchen Ranges. Sheffield plate and cutlery.

Pratt's & Shell Motor Spirit.

High Street, CHIPPENHAM.

Telegrams: "Affleck," Chippenham.   Telephone: 1Y4.

Trade advert for Robert Affleck, who was an ironmonger and supplied agricultural implements, who set up business in 6 High Street in 1901.

ESTABLISHED 1840.

Direct Coal Supply from Colliery to Consumer.   Coal, Coke, Salt, Manure, by Single Truck at Trade Prices.

Depot at Great Western Railway Station, CHIPPENHAM.

| Trade List: SILKSTONE HOUSE. SOMERSETSHIRE. FOREST OF DEAN. STAFFORDSHIRE. DERBYSHIRE and WELSH HOUSE COALS. SMITHS' FOUNDRY and other COALS and COKE. | **F. C. MORTIMORE,** COLLIERY AGENT, Coal, Salt, Cake & Hay Merchant, CHIPPENHAM. Dealer in Artificial Manures, Cattle Food, &c. | Trade List: AGRICULTURAL, ROCK, TABLE and DAIRY SALT, Etc. THORLEY'S CAKE, THORLEY'S LACTIFER. NITRATE OF SODA. GUANA.   BASIC SLAG. PEAT MOSS LITTER. HAY, STRAW, Etc. |

Trade advert for F.C. Mortimore, whose depot was at the rear of the Great Western railway station in roughly 1890. In 1840 Harding & Son opened a new depot for coal, coke, salt and hay alongside the track opposite the station. In 1889 Frederick Mortimore formed a partnership and became the sole owner after Harding's death in the late 1890s. Peter Mortimore took over the business in 1943 until his retirement in 1980, when it was taken over by the Bristol-based Silvey Group. Most of the coal yard is now a car park for the railway station, with only the weigh-bridge and a timber building surviving from the coal yard.

A trade advert for Trotman, the art photographer and Alfred Turpin, who had a photographic warehouse but also specialised in trusses, in around 1890.

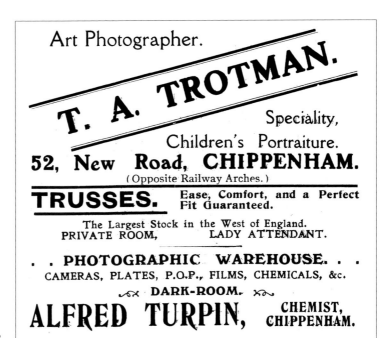

Art Photographer.

T. A. TROTMAN.

Speciality,
Children's Portraiture.

52, New Road, CHIPPENHAM.
(Opposite Railway Arches.)

TRUSSES. Ease, Comfort, and a Perfect Fit Guaranteed.

The Largest Stock in the West of England.
PRIVATE ROOM, LADY ATTENDANT.

. . PHOTOGRAPHIC WAREHOUSE. . .
CAMERAS, PLATES, P.O.P., FILMS, CHEMICALS, &c.
DARK-ROOM.

ALFRED TURPIN, CHEMIST, CHIPPENHAM.

Mr Parry standing at the front of his butcher's shop at 5 The Bridge in 1910.

Ironmonger's shop and displays of W.C. King, who set up business at 52 New Road in 1885.

GARDEN TOOLS & REQUISITES

W. C. KING, IRONMONGER, Oil Merchant, Etc.

NEW ROAD, CHIPPENHAM.

Oil and Coal Stoves for Cooking and Heating purposes.

Travelling Trunks and Bags, Garden Tools and Requisites, Cutlery, Bedsteads, Mangles, Brushes and Mats, etc.

Agents for "Carless," "Pratt's" & "Shell" Motor Spirits, "Kynoch's" Cartridges, etc.

Trade advertisement for W.C. King, ironmonger, *c.* 1890.

Established over a Century. (1785).

BUSSELL, PIKE & WHEELER, CHIPPENHAM.

Corn and Forage Merchants,

Agricultural and Garden Seedsmen.

Cake, Meal, Artificial Manures, Moss Litter, etc.

Telephone 5Y2

Trade advert for Bussell, Pike & Wheeler who set up business in New Road, *c.* 1890.

SEVEN

RAILWAY AND ENGINEERING

View by Bourne along the broad gauge track towards the first Chippenham station, with the open fields of the Ivy estate on the right-hand side, where cows are grazing. The construction of the railway viaduct and embankment caused some disruption to the town and also buried Samborne farmhouse and cut the Old Road. The railway station was not complete when the line was opened in May 1841, until 1858. Records suggest that stone excavated from the Box tunnel in June 1841 was brought back along the line and used to build the station buildings and the railway viaduct. In 1848 the viaduct was widened to accommodate extra tracks.

Chippenham station in June 1899 with the roof cover, which was removed later.

A standard 2-4-0 gauge logo at Chippenham station in the later 1880s. In 1892 the Great Western Railway changed to the narrow gauge of rails. Samples of broad gauge rails are kept in the town's Museum & Heritage Centre and there are still sections of rail around the station and the station car park, used as upright posts.

Looking south west across the fields, towards the station complex on the left and the railway engineering works of Saxby & Farmer, in around 1905.

View of the railway bridge, embankment and station taken from the top of Nestlé chimney, c. 1900.

A portrait of Rowland Brotherhood, who set up his business in 1842 in Chippenham. He took over Silcock's iron foundry on the corner of Langley Road and Foundry Lane and, by the 1850s he was manufacturing railway wagons, switches, crossings and signals for the Great Western Railway.

A portrait of Peter Brotherhood who, under his father Rowland, built about fifteen steam locomotives in the railway works.

An early photograph dated to roughly 1850 showing the expanding railway works, built by Brotherhood.

A picture of one of the saddle tank locomotives, built by Rowland Brotherhood in Chippenham in around 1866.

View of Saxby & Farmer Limited works, taken from the top of St Paul's church spire, *c.* 1910. The previous owner of the works, from 1894, was Evans O'Donnell, who manufactured railway-signalling apparatus.

The assembled workforce of Saxby & Farmer Limited, Chippenham in 1904 or 1905.

The assembled workforce of Saxby & Farmer Limited, Chippenham in around 1910.

Workforce, including young boys, at Saxby & Farmer Limited outside part of the factory, which is being extended due to increased orders. This picture dates from around 1905.

Interior of the planing and shaping section shop, Westinghouse Brake and Signal Company Limited, in around 1926. George Westinghouse established his company in England in 1876 with the original works at King's Cross in London. In 1920 there was a large merger of McKenzie and Holland of Worcester and Saxby Signal Company with Westinghouse Brakes to become the Westinghouse Brake and Signal Company. By 1973 the London office was moved to Chippenham with the works divided into manufacturing divisions of railway, brake and door equipment; signal and mining equipment; automation and control equipment; semi-conductors; rectifier equipment and rapid transit propulsion equipment.

Interior of the lathe shop in Westinghouse Brake and Signal Company Ltd, *c.* 1925.

EIGHT

THE FIRE SERVICE

The Chippenham fire brigade, with their manual fire engine and escape ladder standing in front of Brunel's railway bridge in 1899.

Captain Phipps and other members of the Chippenham fire brigade, with the steam pump, standing in front of the fire station in the Yelde Hall in 1908.

Above left: View of the remains of the Waterford Mill Cloth factory after the disastrous fire of 21 May 1915. *Above right:* View of the burnt out interior of the Waterford Mill Cloth factory showing a fireman using a hooked pole to loosen rubble.

Captain Joe Buckle and the Chippenham firemen posing in the ruins of the Waterford Mill Cloth factory in 1915.

Captain Joe Buckle, back row, left, and other members of the Chippenham brigade, who were winners of the national Fire Brigade's Association competition for steamer, wet class, 1921.

FIRE BRIGADE.

THE CHRISTENING
OF THE
" LEYLAND "
MOTOR FIRE ENGINE

And the handing over of same, accompanied by 1,000 Feet of New Hose, to the CHIPPENHAM TOWN COUNCIL, will take place in the

MARKET PLACE, CHIPPENHAM,

ON SATURDAY, OCT. 21ST, 1922,
AT 3 P.M.

The Ceremony will be preceded by a

PUBLIC LUNCHEON

At the ANGEL HOTEL at 1.30, presided over by CHAS. GARNETT, Esq.

TICKETS 3/6 EACH,

Obtainable from the Officers of the Fire Brigade or at the Angel Hotel.

Poster to commemorate the christening of the new Leyland motor fire engine on Saturday, 21 October 1922. The new engine was a Leyland petrol motor fire engine, which cost £1,500. It replaced the old horse-drawn Victorian Merryweather engine, which still survives and has recently been restored and awaits public display. The money for the new engine was raised by local subscriptions in the town. The capacity of the new engine was 400 gallons of water per minute, which was a marked improvement on the old engine.

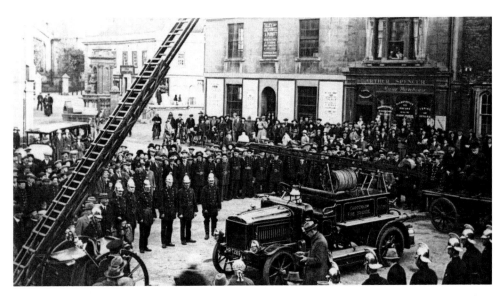

The official christening of the new Leyland motor fire engine at the top end of the Market Place on 21 October 1922.

Captain Joe Buckle and the Chippenham Fire Brigade receiving a commemorative silver jug from Mayor Alderman W. Vince in 1934.

Photograph taken to commemorate the Jubilee celebrations of King George V outside the Yelde Hall fire station in 1935.

NINE

ON THE HOME FRONT

First World War soldiers awaiting goods outside Chippenham railway station in 1916.

Major Justby William Awdry of Chippenham. Original officer of the Second Volunteer
Battalion of the Wiltshire Regiment in about 1910.

Above left: Private Arthur Humphries of the Wiltshire Regiment, who died of his wounds in Salonika on 17 January 1917.

Above right: Photograph of Private Joseph Blanchard, who enlisted in Chippenham, in the 1880s.

Munitions workers in the milling section of Saxby & Farmer Limited during the First World War.

Schoolboys clearing ground for the planting of vegetables, probably at the rear of Woodlands Road, in 1918.

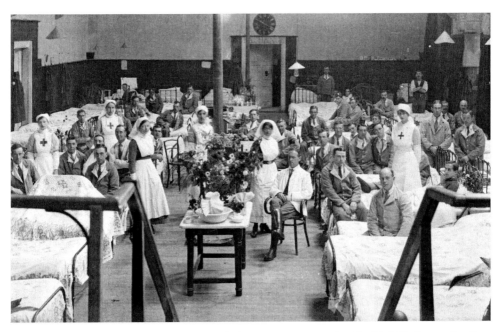

The auxiliary ward of the military hospital that was set up in the Neeld Hall during the First World War.

Wounded soldiers and the nursing staff outside the Neeld Hall, which was the auxiliary military hospital during the First World War.

Munitions workers at Saxby & Farmer Limited, around 1915.

The nursing staff, who tended the wounded soldiers in the auxiliary military hospital in the Neeld Hall in the First World War.

Peace day celebrations in the Neeld Hall on 19 July 1919.

Auxiliary fire squad on 24 November 1940 outside the Chippenham fire station.

German air photograph taken in August 1941 of the Westinghouse Brake and
Signal Company Limited, which was marked for bombing runs.

Guard of honour by E Company First Battalion of the Wiltshire Home Guard for
the visit of Queen Mary to Westinghouse in 1942.

Instruction No. 14

WESTINGHOUSE BRAKE & SIGNAL CO., LTD.

NOTICE

A. R. P.

Smoking in shelters is **STRICTLY PROHIBITED**.

Emergency Exits from the shelters must be used only for the purpose for which they have been installed, and wardens must see that this instruction is adhered to.

18-9-39

H. A. CRUSE,
Works Manager.

Above: ARP notice to staff of the Westinghouse Brake and Signal Company Limited issued after 18 September 1939, referring to bomb shelter rules.

C.1 B

File No. 7/ 5/983

WAR DAMAGE COMMISSION

REGIONAL OFFICE,
4 & 5, WORCESTER ROAD,
CLIFTON,
BRISTOL, 8.

Property 34 Park Avenue

Please keep this slip. It will serve as evidence that you have delivered a notification of damage as required by Section 10 of the War Damage Act, 1941, to the War Damage Commission. It also shows the address of the Regional Office of the Commission by which the notification is held, and the file number relating to your claim. Any correspondence relating to your claim should be addressed to this office and the file number quoted for reference.

F. P. ROBINSON,
Secretary.

Date 18/6/42

M *Simpkins*

Wt. 48597/11 4/41 F.W.W. 51-149

War Damage Commission claim slip referring to bomb damage at 34 Park Avenue, Chippenham.

Ceremony to commemorate VE Day on 8 May 1945, outside the Bear Hotel in the Market Place.

Large crowds assembled in the Market Place for VE Day celebrations on 8 May 1945.

TEN

LIVING IN STYLE

The view of the rear of Orwell House and gardens in New Road, which was occupied by Rowland Brotherhood and his family. The family consisted of eleven sons and three daughters, enabling the father with ten of his sons to field a complete cricket team, which on one occasion they played against eleven members of the Awdry family.

A portrait of Rowland Brotherhood taken in 1877, five years brfore he died. In 1869 he left Chippenham with his business in ruins and was a peniless man, but through hard work he went on to make a new engineering life in Cardiff and Bristol. Before he died in 1882, aged seventy, he wrote his memoirs describing all his achievements in cesspit construction and railway engineering.

A portrait of Priscilla Brotherhood, who gave birth to eleven sons and three daughters.

View of the rear of Clift House in 1906, which was demolished in 1982.

Pew Hill House was built in 1895 by Silcock and Reay, Bath architects, after a design for the owner Miss Dixon. The house is a mixture of both Tudor and Stuart revival.

View of Hardenhuish House in 1908. The house was probably designed as a country mansion by John Wood of Bath, for Joseph Colborne. The house is an example of a rather plain Palladian style with a later curved porch and interior additions by the London architect Sir John Soane.

View of Monkton House, which is an elegant example of a Palladian-style mansion, designed by an unknown architect in the style of John Wood.

ELEVEN

AN EXPANDING TOWN

Looking up Langley Road, *c.* 1900.

View from Langley Road into The Hamlet, *c*. 1900.

Looking along the prosperous, middle-class housing in Marshfield Road in around 1890.

The corner shop being built by Mr Fields in about 1900 on the corner of Park Lane and Malmesbury Road. The builders are posed in front of the partially completed shop with the lashed together wooden scafolding. This corner shop survives and has had many different businesses, a number of which have been connected with both ladies and gentlemens' hairdressing.

Looking up Marshfield Road in 1908 with the West End Club on the right.

Good quality Bath stone-faced houses in Marshfield Road, c. 1900.

The crossroads of Park Lane and Marshfield Road with the West End Club on the right in around 1910.

A very rural Lowden Hill with the vicarage above in around 1910.

Looking along New Road in 1920, late in the evening. The group of workmen are probably going home after working at the newly-created engineering works of Saxby & Farmer.

View along New Road, c. 1890, looking up towards Brunel's railway viaduct. In 1784 John Powell was commissioned by the Council to draw up an accurate map of Chippenham; New Road at this time was not in existence. In 1792 New Road was laid out and late Georgian and Victorian housing was erected. Many of these fine town houses have been converted to shops or demolished.

TWELVE

SPORT

Chippenham Town reserves photographed at the rear of Orwell House in 1899. Back row, standing from left to right: G. Jones; R. Slade (assistant secretary); W. Humphries; H. Garraway; W. Leighfield; H. Harrison; G. Howell; F. Ludgate; H.G. Pinfield (honorary secretary). Middle row: E. Taylor; H. Escott; J. Newman (captain); C. Bacon. Front row: P. Gale; F. Pinfield; F. Bromley; H. Bull; W. Harper.

Members of the Chippenham Tennis Club in the late 1890s.

Chippenham Hockey Club in 1890. Back row from left to right: Sir G. Cater; J. Heatherington; G. Hathaway; -?- ; Sgt Major Lawrence (umpire); E. Neale; P. Gane; Red Steadman; Dr M.S. Wilson. Middle row: -?- ; Mr Napier; W.J. Hiscock; -?- ; Mr Bent; B. Tilley; -?- ; L. Mills; A. Short (groundsman), Mr Laws. Front row: Mr Bailey; Mr Frome; -?- ; Revd Lesley; Mr Pond; T. Hathaway.

Chippenham Town First XI in 1907. Back rows from left to right: G. Curtis
(trainer); A.J. Jones; H. Fouracre; W. Holley; E. Tinson; T. Mustoe; W.H. Bernard;
J. Tinson; A. Light; H. Jones; W. Bennett. Middle row: B. Pinfield (assistant
secretary); B. Escott; A. Boyes; T. Wootton; E. Jones (secretary). Front row: W.
Knight; F.B. Pinfield; A. Duckett; J. Tadd (captain); S. Collier.

Chippenham Rovers Football Club, who were runners up in the Wiltshire League
Division One 1923-24. Back row, left to right: G. Seldon; G. Curtis (trainer); G.
Reckless; H. Bigwood; J. Jones; J. Goddard. Third row: W. Garlick; Dr G. Lawrence
(vice president); H. Roberts (honorary secretary); F. Howell; C. Hemmings; G.
Townsend (captain); S. Reynolds; F. Shave (honorary treasurer); P. Edwards;
G. Dench. Second row: Mrs Bodinnar; J.F. Bodinnar (president); H. Hyman; T.
Bullock; H. Brinkworth; V. Carter; S. Cook (chairman). Front row: J. Bullock; S.
Wood; L. Hunt; H. Emery; A. Bell.

Chippenham Rugby Football Club, winners of the Bath 7-a-side tournament, Colmer Cup, Easter 1936. Back row from left to right: D.C. Royal; A.G. Dunster; T. Rowland; J. Morgan; C. Lewis. Middle row: B. Henson; R.P. Royal; R.J. Cole; R. Henson; R.C. Sharp; C. Robinson. Front row: C. Weston; A.H. Heath; J. Powell; K.J. Post (captain); A.J. Lucas; W.J. Bassett; M.J. Hathaway.

THIRTEEN

ROYAL VISITS
AND EVENTS

Celebrations in the Market Place for the Jubilee of Queen Victoria in 1897.

Diamond Jubilee bonfire and the building committee, 22 June 1897.

The royal visitors leaving Chippenham railway station to embark on their visit to the town in 1907.

The visit of King Edward VII to Chippenham on 20 July 1907, showing the decorations erected in honour of the visit.

Decoration on the steps of the Town Hall for the accession of George VI in 1937.

Street decorations hanging from Brunel's railway bridge for the coronation of King George VI in 1937.

FOURTEEN

PEOPLE

Simon Downing was the co-founder of Downing and Rudman, the building business which was established in 1830 in the Old Road. Simon carried on his father's business and the company became well known for the quality of its wood carving, particularly in church buildings. Kelly's Directory of 1931 describes them as 'specialists in oak work and medieval iron work and the complete renovation of ancient buildings.' Some of their more important woodcarvings can be seen on Worcester Cathedral and Battle Abbey. In 1936 Edward Bent bought the company, who are now known as Downing, Rudman and Bent. During the Second World War the company built RAF and military establishments. The company's offices and workshops are in Spanbourne Avenue and are still actively engaged in high quality carpentry. Simon is sitting outside the front of his house in St Mary's Street. He was the last man to be buried in St Andrew's churchyard.

Wedding group of the Davies family 22 May 1909 in the garden of Westmead House behind the Tanyard, Chippenham. The Davies family occupied Westmead House, which was surrounded by well-kept gardens as can be glimpsed in the picture. With the closure of the tanyard the house and gardens were also demolished and became part of Flowers scrapyard. The area is now vacant and about to be redeveloped and will again be used, certainly in part, for domestic housing and gardens.

Alderman Edward Swayne, mayor in 1924 and 1935, along with the mayoress and Harry Milsom, mace-bearer in the Town Hall, 1935.

Two suffragettes standing on their soapbox in front of their mobile caravan with the slogans of 'Votes for Women', meeting at Chippenham in the Market Place prior to 1914. A large crowd, which seems to be mostly male judging from the types of hats on display, is seen looking up and listening to their speeches. It is not known who the suffragettes were and no record has been discovered of their meeting in Chippenham that day in the press.

FIFTEEN

INNS AND TAVERNS

The Rose & Crown public house in about 1880. The inn is first mentioned in 1691 and was probably built of timber, some of which can be seen behind brickwork and stonework on the sides and rear of the building. As the inn backed onto the canal basin, it was the nearest 'watering hole' for the canal people.

The Great Western Hotel in New Road in about 1877, which was demolished when the new underpass was constructed.

The Five Alls Inn in the Causeway in 1908, which was relocated to Sheldon Road in 1937. The Five Alls were: 'I rule all, I pray for all, I plead for all, I fight for all, I pay for all'.

The Royal Oak Inn in the 1890s, with George Stokes as landlord. The inn is first mentioned in a document of 1835.

The Angel Hotel in around the 1900s with the mail coach waiting to leave. The Angel in 1613 was called the Bull and it was not until 1747 that it was re-named the Angel. The Angel has recently been internally renovated. The motel behind was built by the architect R.J. Brown in 1959. The motel is possibly one of the earliest to be built in this country; this has now been demolished and replaced with an extension to the hotel.

The Three Crowns in London Road in about 1918 with a shepherd and his flock. This inn is first recorded in documents in 1784.

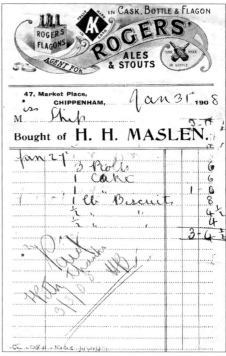

Above left: Label for cider produced by the Lion Brewery in the Market Place, Chippenham.
Above right: Letterhead for Rogers' Ales and Stouts, 47 Market Place, 1908.